Joseph Doddridge

**Logan**

The Last of the Race of Shikellemus

Joseph Doddridge

**Logan**
*The Last of the Race of Shikellemus*

ISBN/EAN: 9783337336455

Printed in Europe, USA, Canada, Australia, Japan

Cover: Foto ©Thomas Meinert / pixelio.de

More available books at **www.hansebooks.com**

# LOGAN,

THE LAST OF THE RACE OF

## Shikellemus, Chief of the Cayuga Nation.

## A DRAMATIC PIECE.

TO WHICH IS ADDED

The Dialogue of the Backwoodsman and the Dandy,

First Recited at the Buffaloe Seminary, July the 1st, 1821.

### By Dr. JOSEPH DODDRIDGE.

Reprinted from the Virginia Edition of 1823, with an

APPENDIX RELATING TO THE MURDER OF LOGAN'S FAMILY

FOR

WILLIAM DODGE.
BY ROBERT CLARKE & CO.
CINCINNATI.
1868.

# LOGAN.

### THE LAST OF THE RACE OF SHIKELLEMUS CHIEF OF THE CAYUGA NATION.

## A DRAMATIC PIECE.

#### TO WHICH IS ADDED,
#### THE DIALOGUE OF THE BACKWOODSMAN,
#### AND THE DANDY,
#### FIRST RECITED AT THE BUFFALOE SEMINARY,
*July* the 1st 1821.

### BY Dr. JOSEPH DODDRIDGE.

---

--"Moriamur, et in media arma ruamus,
UnaSalus victis, nullam sperare salutem."

---

BUFFALOE CREEK: BROOKE COUNTY, VA.
PRINTED FOR THE AUTHOR, BY SOLOMON SALA, AT
THE BUFFALOE PRINTING OFFICE.

1823.

# PREFACE.

In collecting materials for the notes on the settlement and wars of the western country, the history of the unfortunate Cayuga chief Logan presented itself. I thought his bravery, talents, and misfortunes worthy of a dramatic commemoration. For attempting the task of doing justice to the character of Logan, I have no apology to make. My right to the use of the pen, and press is equal to that of any other man. Of the public I shall ask no indulgence. The imperial court of public opinion decides on the merit of every literary work, without favor or malice.

If the work is well written it will live; if not it will go where it ought, to the shades of oblivion. In the latter case however one advantage will result from my attempt, I shall have furnished materials for some abler hand to perform a work which certainly is due to the world.

The tear of commiseration is due to Logan. Like Wallace, he outlived the independence of his nation. Like Cato, he "greatly fell with his falling state." Like Ossian, he was the last of his family, all of whom, but himself, had fallen by assassinations, which, for their atrocious character, are scarcely paralleled in history.

"In every period of society, human manners are a curious spectacle."* The drama professes to represent them, and, when faithful to its object, cannot fail to be interesting. How far I

*Blair.

have succeeded in giving a correct portrait of the manners of the period of time alluded to, in the following composition, must be left to the judgment of the reader. As it respects the Backwoods-men, I cannot be wrong, for I was brought up among them, and, I trust, that I have done justice to the customs and phraseology of the native sons of our forests. In all its historical allusions it is strictly correct.

Should it be said that the piece, as to the characters which it represents, is too horrible for the stage, or that its form is improper theatrical representation, I would willingly acquiesce in the decision, as I have no great ambition to appear in that department. It is enough that it be read; but if unworthy of that, why, then, let it be thrown aside, among other abortive productions of the pen, and press.

# THE ARGUMENT.

Logan, the principal subject of the following dramatic composition, was the second son of Shikellemus, a famous Chief of the Cayuga nation, whose residence was at Shamokin on the Susquehana. He was a man of peace, much attached to the English government, and of great service in bringing about the peace between the Indians and the Whites in the fall of 1764. Logan followed his father's example, till the spring of 1774, when the atrocious and unprovoked murders of the Indians, at the mouth of Captina, on the 27 of April; and at the mouth of big Yellow Creek, on the third day afterwards, and which comprehended the whole of Logan's family, brought on the war of the Earl of Dunmore, which ended in the peace of Camp Charlotte, in November, in the same year. This drama, therefore, embraces a period of about seven months.

It is reported that Logan, after the peace became melancholy and intemperate, and often wished for death; and that he was murdered somewhere between Detroit and the Miami, but by whom, or on what account, is not at present known.

## DRAMATIS PERSONÆ.

Capt. Furioso.
1 Lieutenant.
2 Lieutenant.
Capt. Pacificus.
Logan, Chief of the Cayugas.
Shahillas, Chief of the Ottoways.
Tawatwees, Chief of the Shawnees.
Kuhn, Chief of the Wyandots, a prisoner to Logan.
Queeta, an old Squaw.
Sheba, son of Queeta.
Tawasta and Neputa, Daughters of Queeta.
Officers, Militia men, warriors, spies, messengers, and interpreters.

# LOGAN.

## ACT I.

SCENE I.—*Wheeling. A Militia Council of War.*

*Capt. Furioso.* The Indians are gathering close about us: what shall we do with them?

1st *Lieutenant.* Let us fall to work, and kill every rascal of them without delay, for they certainly intend mischief.

2d *Lieutenant.* What evidence have we that they design to do mischief?

1st *Lieut.* Have you not heard of their having stolen horses from the land jobbers, and that they have killed nearly all the traders that were among them?

2d *Lieut.* I have heard these reports; but do not know thro' what channel they come. Perhaps they may not be true: a few days will confirm the truth or falsehood of them. We had therefore better wait a while.

1st *Lieut.* I am for no delay. You know that even a false report is always followed by a true one of the same kind. If the Indians have not already done mischief, they will soon do it.

2d *Lieut.* I am no prophet. I cannot forsee what these Indians intend doing.

*Capt. Fur.* I am afraid that evil is gathering about us, or why so large an encampment of Indians at the mouth of Yellow

Creek? Another has been made at the mouth of Captina. Thus they are stationed both above and below us, and more of them are now coming down the river in canoes. What do these things mean? Why do these Yellow-jackets come so near us?

 2d *Lieut.* They are still on their own ground.

 1st *Lieut.* On their own ground! What ground can an Indian have? I would as soon apply to a buffaloe, for a right to the land over the river, as to an Indian. I could prove that he marked the earth with his feet, had eaten the weeds and brushed the bushes with his tail, and made paths to the salt licks, and what has an Indian done more?

 *Capt. Fur.* An Indian is not worthy to be compared to a buffaloe: He is a wolf, or bear, that lives upon the destruction of everything about him. He is a beast of prey.

 2d *Lieut.* They have at least the right of possession to the country. Providence placed them here, long before the white people knew anything of this quarter of the earth.

 *Capt. Fur.* That is true, and if they had been worthy of its possession, they would have been continued in it; but they are Canaanites, whom Providence has doomed to utter extermination.

 2d *Lieut.* I am no Moses, and am therefore not authorized to pass this dreadful sentence upon them.

 *Capt. Fur.* Neither am I a Moses; but I am a Joshua to execute the decree of their destruction, and altho' I cannot command the sun and moon to stand still; yet if my companions think as I do, this very day shall be long enough to finish some of them.

 *Capt. Pacificus.* Perhaps we had better take a little time for deliberation on this weighty concern. The Indians are not likely to leave their present encampments shortly, and we shall soon find means to discover their intentions.

*Capt. Fur.* What, shall we wait for the tomahoc and scalping-knives, of the Indians to convince us of their bad intentions! Are you not aware that they claim the very ground on which we stand? At the conclusion of the war between the English and the French, in 1763, they entered into a confederacy to destroy all the forts, and settlements in the western country, and nearly did so. Have you forgotten the slaughter at Shamokin, and those of Muddy Creek, and the Big-levels, in the Greenbrier country?

*Capt. Pac.* I am well acquainted with the history of those events, and also with the doings of the Paxton Boys, in murdering the Canestoga Indians in the jail of Lancaster. (Pa.) Depend upon it, if we have ground of complaint against the Indians; they are not without theirs against us. We ought not to be too hasty in this affair.

1st *Lieut.* The Paxton Boys did right. An Indian ought to be killed, he is naturally a murderer, and if not at war, it is only because he is chained down by fear.

2d *Lieut.* They have been at peace with us for ten years. We are now much stronger than we were ten years ago, and I do not see any thing at present to encourage them to go to war against us.

*Capt. Fur.* I am afraid you do not perfectly understand the matter. The Indians have much to encourage them to go to war: they know as well as we do, that we are shortly to have war with the English, and they will join them. I believe they have done so already, and that the English at Detroit, are now supplying them with arms, and ammunition.

1st *Lieut.* I know we shall have war: Did we not all see the great lights in the north last winter. They looked like ranks of soldiers, and troops of horsemen. Sometimes I thought I could see the flashes of the guns. The dogs have howled every night for a long time past. A few nights ago I dreamed that I saw a black cloud coming slowly from the westward; when it came over my house it gathered into a bunch, fell down into the yard, and turned into blood. The blood appeared to be ancle deep. These we all know are signs of war, and we shall have it. We had better strike the first blow.

*Capt. Pac.* Northern lights, dogs, and dreams, are not good foundations for war. If the council were disposed to hear them, I could give the most satisfactory proofs that the Indians do not intend war at this time.

2d *Lieut.* Let us hear them.

*Capt. Pac.* In all their encampments on the Ohio we do not hear of any war Chiefs being among them. This is never the case when they intend war. In the time of hostilities they are more obedient to their Chiefs than we are, and do nothing without their advice.

The absence of their Chiefs is an evidence that their intentions are not hostile.

At their encampments on the Ohio, there are more women and children, than men; if they intended to make war, this would not be the case. Whenever the Indians make war, they remove their women and children to a place of safety, as we do ours. If we are to have war, let us not sneak into it, like a thief in the night. If the presence of these Indians along the river is disagreeable to us, let us tell them so. In that case no doubt they will remove farther off; if not, there will be some pretext for hostilities against them.

*Capt. Fur.* I am for no delay. Let us strike while the iron is hot. They are within our reach, and we ought not to let them escape.

*Capt. Pac.* Surely you will not kill women and children. This would be not only inhuman, but dishonorable.

*Capt. Fur.* I would kill all, nits will be lice; they have killed the traders, and now blood for blood. No mercy ought to be shown to them.

*Capt. Pac.* We do not know that they have killed any traders; and if they have they were not within our jurisdiction, so that we are under no obligation to avenge their deaths. If traders, from a motive of gain, choose to venture among them, let them abide by the consequence. We have nothing to do with them.

1st *Lieut.* I am for avenging the blood of any white man shed by the Indians.

*Capt. Pac.* Does it then belong to you or me, to make war or peace? Peace and war, are national concerns, and not those of individuals. If the Indians have committed murders, let us ascertain the facts, and report them to the government. A negotiation will follow, and if satisfaction be not given, a declaration of war will be the consequence: We can then go to war openly, and with a good conscience.

*Capt. Fur.* I am for no delay. I will not wait for a declaration of war.

*Capt. Pac.* What then? Will you be a murderer. Will you attack and slaughter people who are at peace? If you intend any such thing let them know it, that they may have an equal chance with you. Do not take them by surprise. Be an honorable soldier. A murderer is a coward. Besides, by killing these people you would become answerable to the criminal justice of our country.

1st *Lieut.* The criminal justice of our country, for killing Indians! We are not afraid of that. All the sheriffs, magistrates and constables in the country could not take one of us. If they should attempt it we would soon shew them the effects of club law.

*Capt. Fur.* The thing must be done this very day. There are many of us who have lost relations in the former war, by the hand of Indians, and their bones are not yet buried. Now we have a chance to bury them, and we must do it. Our people will be much disappointed if we do not strike the blow. Let us be off.

*Capt. Pac.* I have something more to say to you before the council breaks up.

*Capt. Fur.* We are ready to hear you, provided you do not detain us too long. The day is wearing away, and we have a great deal to do. This is to be the day of vengeance.

*Capt. Pac.* A day of vengeance truly! More so I apprehend than you are aware of. It may be a piece of sport to you, to shoot these Indian men, and bury the tomahoc in the heads of their women and children.

1st *Lieut.* Aye. This is the very game we want to be at, and that forthwith.

*Capt. Pac.* But will business end here? Will you murder our own people too?

*Capt. Fur.* What do you mean by this question?

*Capt. Pac.* I will explain myself. The moment you strike the blow war is declared, and you may rest assured the Indians will not be slow in making retaliation; but are we now in a condition to go to war? We have had ten years of peace, during which time the country has been settled pretty smartly, but still the population is but thin, and we are all poor, we have no army, but few arms, and little ammunition to help ourselves with. You know our men had better be at work, and raise corn, and get meat to keep their families from starving, than to spend their time in building forts and going on scouts, and campaigns, this is not the worst, more than one half of our people will leave the country. Strike this blow, immediately every road leading to the mountains and over them, will be crowded with families flying from the war. Your residence Capt. is not among us. You can easily return home, and there you will be out of danger. Will you light up the flames of war and then leave the few who, either cannot, or will not leave the country to contend with it?

*Capt. Fur.* Do you suppose I am afraid of danger? I shall be amongst you.

*Capt Pac.* That may be; or may not be. To tell you the honest truth, I think but little of the bravery of any man who can ever harbor a thought of committing murder in cold blood. At all events, the man who can kill a woman or child, must be a coward.

*Capt. Fur.* Do you mean that I am a coward, and that I intend to commit murder?

*Capt. Pac.* I do not intend to retract anything that I have said, take it as you like. I had much rather risk a shot with you, than suffer you to do what you intend, if I could prevent it. I have but one life to lose, and you may as well take it, if you can, as that I should lose it in a war which you are about to bring on, and this will likely be my fate, as I intend at all events, to abide by the stuff.

1st *Lieut.* No more of that we have other matters on hand.

*Capt. Pac.* I know very well that I am in no danger from you, say what I may. But I feel for others. What torrents of blood must be shed in consequence of what you are about to do this day! On you, and on your party, be the blame of the widows, and orphans, whose husbands, and fathers, must soon perish by the savages, in revenge for their relations, and friends, whom you are about to slaughter. Their sighs, their tears, and their poverty, will be laid to your account. To the latest posterity your names will be stained with blood. You will be regarded as cowards, and murderers, who have involved your country in a destructive war, without provocation—Would to God the Indians were acquainted with your design, that they might give you the reception you so richly deserve, and prevent the bloodshed of innocent people.

*Capt. Fur.* You had better give them notice then.

*Capt. Pac.* Were it in my power I certainly should do so; but you know it is not.

*Capt. Fur.* Let us put the matter to vote at once, we have talked too long already. If anything is to be done, let us do it. Call in our men.

### SCENE II.

*Enter a number of Militia, dressed in their habit, with rifles in their hands.*

*Capt. Fur.* Men what have you to say about those Indians along the river? shall we kill them; or let them alone?

*Omnes.* Kill them. Kill them. Men, women, and children. Let us not leave one of them alive.

1st *Lieut.* The majority governs. Our resolution is taken. To work then my brave boys as speedily as possible.

[*Exeunt omnes.*

*Capt. Pac.* Oh! Lord what is man? Is he thine image here below? Is he the son of reason? Why then is he the victim of the vilest passions! He boasts of a revelation of thy divine government, teaching him to be the good Samaritan; yet he is a fury. With all the rewards of a good conscience and the divine favor before him, he riots in the blood of his fellow man with savage brutality. What is there of justice on our side in the contest which must follow the deeds of this day? We have ravished their country from these sons of the forest, and now slaughter them without provocation. What is the life of man? It is like that of the frail mushroom, short in itself, yet liable to premature destruction by the tread of every foot. O! my country what a waste of life is soon to take place among our people, who although poor, were 'till now, peaceful, and contented. God of justice! I call thee to witness that in the murderous deeds of this day, I have had no participation, and I invoke thy protection for me, and mine, during the storm of war now impending over us!

## ACT II.

SCENE I.—*The council house at Sandusky, enter the chiefs Logan, Shahillas, Tawatwees and Kuhn—a number of death halloos, in succession, at a distance.*

*Logan.* Bad news. What can this mean?
*Shahillas.* We shall soon hear. What eight deaths?
*Enter Messenger.*
What news brother?
*Mes.* Bad news—the long knives have made war and killed some of our people.

*Log.* Where?

*Mes.* Two in a canoe above Wheeling and six more at Captina.

*Tawatwees.* Can you tell the reason of their having done so.

*Mes.* No—we had not offended them: when they were coming to our camp we thought them friends, 'till they fired upon us, and killed six of our people.

*Tawa.* For some time past I thought we should have war.* We have seen great lights in the north. The owls have been very plenty, and the pidgeons scarce. I have seen a great many strange sights, and heard strange noises in the air; yet I have always rejoiced in the sun beam of peace.

*Kuhn.* The life of man is a life of war. The wolves cannot eat grass. Something must die before they can eat. The fox kills and eats the harmless birds. The rattle snake has its poison, and its teeth. The eagle has its claws, and its strong bill. Every thing about us is at war, and can we expect peace? No! we must soon be at war. Such is the will of the great spirit. These white people are as fond of blood as we are. They have dipped their hands in the blood of our people, and we must do so with theirs. The great father of the white people over the great water is angry with his children and will soon make war upon them, to punish them for being too proud, and we must join the great father. He has guns, powder, and lead for us, in exchange for our skins, and fur; but his children are poor, and have nothing for themselves.

*Sha.* Let us not be too fast. This news has come to us like a bolt of thunder. The news has made our ears deaf, and the flash has blinded our eyes. We are like a man just awakening out of sleep, at the dawn of the morning, while the light is not

---

*The Aurora borealis was a common occurrence for several winters preceding the commencement of the revolutionary war.

yet clear, and his eyes not yet quite awake. He thinks he sees a bunch of large trees; but they are nothing but a bunch of bushes. He sees, as he thinks, a large mountain; but it is only a little hill. The grass of the prearie he mistakes for a large water. Brothers let us listen a little longer before we lift the hatchet.

[*A number of death halloos in succession at a distance.*]

*Logan*, counting the halloos. What, twelve more dead!

*Enter Messenger.*

*Log.* You bring us bad news brother.

*Mes.* Very bad! The long knives have killed twelve of our people at Yellow creek.

*Kuhn.* They are for war. They are in earnest.

*Log.* Can you tell me what has become of my people?

*Mes.* They are all dead. Some of them at Captina, and the rest at Yellow creek. In the morning the captain of the white men came over to our camp, and looked very sharply about. I believe he counted us. Your sister told him to go away. That the Indians were angry, because their friends down the river had been killed. He went away. Afterwards your brother, and sister, and some more went over the river to the house where they sold rum to the Indians—but they took no guns with them. After they had been there a while, the white men killed them all. Several more were killed in a canoe as they were going over the river to see what had happened.

*Log.* Logan is left alone; but he will not weep. He will think only of revenge. What think you brothers, must we not cover the blood of our people?

*Kuhn.* The red hatchet must be lifted. Our arms must be strong for war. Call in the peace chiefs.

## SCENE II.

*\*Enter Wingemind, and some other peace chiefs.*

*Taw.* † For ten snows and ten ears of corn you have governed our nations. The light was clear all about us. Our war posts are fallen down and rotten. The scalp-halloo has not been heard. Our young men can hardly make it. A dark cloud is now coming from the place where the sun wakes up in the morning. You must leave the storm to us; only the good weather belongs to you.

*Peace Chiefs.* Let us first hear all you have to say, before we consent to exchange the clear light, for darkness, and the sun shine, and sweet little winds, for thunder, and storms.

*Sha.* Let us think a little before we strike. The panther before he springs on his prey, takes time to squat down, fix his claws, and mark his exact course with his eyes. The snake before he bites, rattles, and coils himself up.

*Taw.* We must have war. The bones of our friends must be covered.

*Sha.* Must they be covered with the war hatchet? Brothers it may be that in attempting to do this, we may leave our bones uncovered with theirs.

*Kuhn.* We are warriors. We must be strong.

*Sha.* We are not strong; although we are good warriors ourselves, and so are our men; but we are few in number, and we are poor. These white people are like an ant-hill, you may tear

---

\* The Indians have two sets of chiefs, one for war and the other for peace. When war is declared, the peace chiefs are out of place, and the war chiefs have the command. When peace is made, the peace chiefs resume the government.

† The Indian terms for Summer and Winter.

down a part of it, and kill a great many; but there are always enough left to build it up again, and the dead are not missed.

*Log.* The spirit of our friends will never rest until we have revenge on the whites. They have killed my people and I must kill too.

*Sha.* My heart is sorry for you, brother Logan. You have no brother to hunt with you, you have no wife, and sister to take care of your cabbin, and plant your corn. Were I angry at Logan I would say that he, as well as his grand father, *Shikellemus* has been too fond of the white skins; but we all do wrong sometimes. Logan is our brother, and his people were ours too. We must take part in his revenge; but brothers, I think we had best wait for a better opportunity.

*Kuhn.* What better opportunity shall we ever have? Shall we ever be stronger than we are now? Will the great spirit put the thunder, and lightning into our hands, and tell us to dash them upon the white skins? will he turn rocks, and bushes into Indians, to help us in the war? He has not told us so. We must have revenge, or give up, and say that we are squaws. Now is the time to strike, unless brother Shahillas knows something we do not.

*Sha.* It takes time to prepare for war. We might now strike a blow, and kill a great many before these white men would be ready for war. Yes brother Logan might have revenge for the blood of his people in a short time. His bullets, and tomahoc might soon cover their bones deep in the ground; but brothers listen! Our squaws must first be taken to a safe place, or the scouts of the white people would soon reach and kill them all, and where shall we put them? would Sandusky, Coshocton, or Chillicothe be far enough from them? would they not sooner find them at all these towns?

*Taw*. I am for revenge at once. The bones of our people must be covered. I am not afraid to die. I can die but once, and no matter how soon if I have made satisfaction to the spirits of my murdered friends. The large snake rattles, and bites, altho' he knows he is to be killed the next moment; but he dies contentedly, because he has struck his enemy the first blow, so will Tawatwees, if the great spirit says it shall be so.

*Kuhn*. The white people have already drove the red men from the long shore of the great water, where the sun rises, across the Allegheny mountains, and now over the Ohio. Many nations on the other side of the great mountain who used to count thousands, have vanished from the earth like the fog along the rivers in a summer morning. Others not quite gone are now small, and their legs are cut off so that they cannot fight. They are not satisfied yet. They must have our country too. Do we not see the marks of their hatchets on the trees? their honey flies have come among us, and we shall see them with their iron strings,* measuring off our land for themselves. Brothers, if the white people must have our country, let us make it cost them as much of their blood as we can spill.

*Sha*. Brother Kuhn has said that the white men will not be long at peace. That their great father is angry with them. This I believe from things I have heard among them at Detroit. There will be but one ear of corn, and one snow more before they lift the red hatchet. We will then join our great father. We shall then be like a little bush under the shelter of a large tree, whose great arms cover it from the storms. By ourselves we are like a boy whose arms are not yet strong enough for the war; but by the side of our great father, we shall be strong enough for the white men.

---

* Surveyor's chain.

If we should strike now they will come from the other side of the great mountain where the sun rises, like swarms of locusts. They will cut roads through our country for the carriage of their big rifles, which make thunder, and lightning; and they will fall on us with their long rows of men with coats all of one colour, with one horned guns in their hands. Shahillas is not afraid; but he wishes to wait 'till he becomes stronger before he strikes the blow.

*Log.* Logan has been called the friend of the white men: his great father Shikellemus taught him to be so; but Logan is still an Indian, and he must have blood for blood. The spirits of his friends cannot rest until he has taken revenge. If none will join Logan he will go alone, and kill till his arm is sick. He will fear no danger. Why should he fear? when he falls there is none left to mourn for his death.

*Taw.* We must join our brother Logan. He shall not fall alone. We must fight and die with him. Let the war-post be set deep in the ground.

*Kuhn.* Our brothers have already raised the war-post.

*Log.* How many have struck it with their hatchets?

*Kuhn.* Every man. They are all warriors. Let us call them, and tell them to prepare for the war dance.

*Enter the young warriors.*

*Taw.* Young men you have been raised in the sun shine of peace; but now comes the storm of war. You have killed the deer, buffaloe, and elk, now you must kill white men. The bones of our friends are not covered, you must cover them deep in the ground with the red hatchet.

*Sha.* Shahillas thought it too soon to strike the white men; but the other chiefs say now is the time. Shahillas is not afraid.

Logan must have revenge for the loss of his friends, and we must strike with him. The young men have said all to me, shew us the white men, and we will kill them. I will shew you the white men, and if any turn his back upon them in battle, he shall die by my hands. You wish for war, now you shall fight.

*War song of the Chiefs.*

Ye peace chiefs retire, for your sunshine is o'er.
Your reign has been mild, as the breezes of spring.
The clouds gather round us, and peace is no more,
'Till the strife of our warriors, a conquest shall bring.

Young men, who have grown in the mild beam of peace,
In hunting, and singing, the feast, and the dance,
Must now become warriors; and give up the chase,
In revenge for the dead, like a whirlwind advance.

Their spirits now call you to cover their bones
From the clouds they invite you to vengeance in blood.
O! quick put an end to their grief and their groans,
Your fathers command it, and call the deed good.

*Response of the Young Warriors.*

We'll haste to the land, where our people have bled,
The red hatchet of war, for their death shall atone,
The white man shall sink to his cold clayey bed;
And our fathers approve the brave deed of their sons.

[*Exeunt Chiefs and Warriors.* LOGAN *solus.*]

*Log.* Logan is left alone, the last of a long race of Chiefs renowned in peace, and in war, which when he dies, like the shooting star, will leave no track behind. The spring has come; but

# LOGAN.

Logan has none to plant corn for him. The flowers appear on the vallies, and hills; but they have no fragrance for Logan. Logan smells nought but blood. The birds sing in the groves; but they sing not for Logan. Logan will hear nought but the war whoop, and the death halloo. The swallows, and robin red breasts, and bats have awoke from their long death of sleep. The wild geese, and swans have returned from the south, to hatch their young on the shores of the lakes, pairs of little birds in the fulness of love, are building their nests, the green leaves are breaking from their buds, the grass, and weeds begin to wave in the wind, all things are full of life, but Logan dies, and with him all his race. Logan lives only for revenge.

## ACT III.

SCENE I.—*Council House at Chillicothe.*

*Kuhn, Tawatwees and others in Council.*

[*Enter Shahillas.*

*Kuhn.* What news brother?

*Sha.* Bad indeed! We have been defeated by the long knives, where we felt sure of a victory.

*Taw.* You make our hearts sore; but we must hear all the bad news; tell us how the red men were beaten, they are strong.

*Sha.* We thought to have reached the mouth of Kenhawa, before the long knives, and to make a hard blow on the settlements on its upper branches; but they were there the day before us. The evening before the battle, we held a council. I proposed to go over the river and make peace with the white men; but my men would fight, and Shahillas must command. We crossed the river and the battle began next morning, at waking up of the sun. Our warriors made their line from the Ohio to the Kenhawa. The long knives were in the forks of the river. For a while we beat them; but a great number of them came out from their camp, and we were defeated. Our warriors are coming home in small parties, to keep themselves from starving. Brothers we have fought bravely. We have done our duty; but we are too weak for the white men.

*Taw.* You bring us bad news indeed. Shahillas told us before the war began that we are too weak for the white men; and Shahillas is not weak. He is a warrior, and I am afraid he is a prophet too; but Tawatwees still hopes that the great spirit will not forsake his red children. The darkest and the coldest time is just before the sun wakes up in the morning. The light may shine around us yet.

*Sha.* It is in vain to hope that we shall be strong enough to fight with the long knives. The fawn cannot fight with the wolf, the young bird with the rattle snake, or the pidgeon with the eagle. The white men are many in number; we are but few. They are rich; we are poor. They know everything; we know nothing—they can do every thing; we can do but little. When things begin to run their course, they will go on 'till they reach their end. Brothers can we stop the winds from blowing? can we say to the lightning go no farther? can we make the clouds hold up the rain? We are going down the hill, and we must go to the bottom. These white men have driven our people from the sea shore to the Ohio. They will soon have this country, and drive us on to the place where the sun sleeps, 'till there shall be no place for hunting, or raising corn. If the great spirit say it shall be so, we cannot help it.

*Kuhn.* Shall we then say that our legs have been cut off so that we cannot fight? Shall we submit our breast to the bullets, and our heads to the tomahocs of the long knives? Must we become squaws and beg them not to kill us?

*Sha.* No Brothers we must make a good peace with them, or fight to the last. If they must have our blood, we must sell it to them for as much of theirs as we can get. Brothers we must answer to our fathers for the deeds of our lives. Our misfortunes are not our faults. Ought a tree to be blamed when split to pieces by the thunder? Is it the fault of the little fawn that he is eaten up by the wolf; or the harmless bird that he is swallowed by the snake? Time makes, and destroys every thing. We see the big bones about our licks; where shall we now find the race of beasts to which they belonged? They are all gone. Do we not walk every day over the bones of a race of men who have vanished from the earth, like white clouds in the evening? Who built the great graves and forts which are seen all over our country? Perhaps they were killed by our forefathers. The whites will destroy us. We have had our day, our night is at hand. These white men will have theirs, and then some strong nation will bring the dark night upon them. So says the great spirit. His arm is strong we cannot hold it. We have only to do the best we can, where he has put our feet.

(*Several scalp-halloos at a distance.*)

*Taw.* Good news! It is like the clear sun shine after dark clouds and heavy rains.

*Sha.* The news although good must be but little. It will be to us like the first morning light to a man sick of a fever, whose pulse beats too hard in his temples, he rejoices to see the light, but is still sick. It is like a good plaister on a spider.* The

---

* Spider is the Indian name for a cancer.

pain is stopped a little time; but his legs are too long to be pulled out, he holds fast, and bites 'till the man dies.

(*The scalp halloos continue.*)

*Taw.* It is the voice of Logan.

*Kuhn.* He cames with his hatchet red with blood. His scalps on a large stick, and I hope with a prisoner for the fire.

*Taw.* (*Pointing thro' a crack in the council house*) I see him yonder: he has a prisoner.

*Kuhn.* Thank the great spirit.

## SCENE II.

*Enter Logan with three warriors, bringing a prisoner, and three scalps on a pole.*

*Log.* Good brother (*Shakes hands with all the Chiefs*) I have covered some of the blood of my people (*presents the prisoner and scalps*).

*Kuhn.* Our hearts are glad brother, that the great spirit has given success to the red hatchet of war in your hand. You have been strong, though before now always the friend of peace.

*Log.* Logan was the son of peace; but now he has tasted blood, peace will never live in Logan's cabbin again.

*Taw.* Young warriors take away the prisoner, make him run the gauntlet, tie him to a stake, make his white skin as black as a burnt tree, with powder and water, kindle the fire. We will then tell you what is to be done.

*Exeunt warriors with the prisoner.*

*Kuhn.* Shall we burn the prisoner?

*Taw.* I think so. It is now a long time since our old warriors have smelt the burning flesh of a white man. Our young warriors have never seen a prisoner burned at the stake. They must see what their fathers have so often seen. Their hearts are too soft, they must be made harder. Let them burn the prisoner, and let some of the old men shew them how to do it, that he may not die too soon.

*Sha.* What shall we gain by burning the prisoner? I cannot see that burning him will be of any service to us. He is a prisoner and cannot help himself, *Shahillas* is a warrior, and will never lay his hand upon the helpless, and weak; unless in mercy. He will give him food if he is hungry, and clothe him if he is ragged, but he will not kill him; if he did, he would shoot him; but not burn him.

*Kuhn. Shahillas* is a warrior. In battle he is a storm, his heart is strong, death follows the blow of his hatchet, and the flash of his gun; but when the fight is over he is as mild as the little winds in the spring. He can take a prisoner; but cannot kill him after he is in his hands? *Shahillas* is too good.

*Taw.* This war was made for revenge, and we must have it. If our lives should pay for it. War is not the work of kindness. We must shoot, stab, tomahoc, and burn all the whites we can catch. War is the work of death. So the long knives treat the red skins. The men, women, and children are all alike to them. If the little child cries, they dont mind it, they break its head with the tomahoc. They know more than we do, and ought be better than they are. Let us burn him.

*Sha.* This war cannot last many moons longer. Burning this prisoner will only make it worse. This prisoner has friends, perhaps his blood runs in the veins of more than one hundred people, if we burn him they must kill too, and where will our murders come to an end? This prisoner looks like a man who has a good head and heart and is a big man among his people. Kindness to him may be kindness to ourselves in the end. Let us not burn him.

*Kuhn.* Burning prisoners has been the custom of our forefathers from old times, and their spirit will be angry with us if we depart from their custom. Do we not see bones mixed with coals, and ashes on the graves. It was on the top of those little hills, which they made with their own hands, that they burned their prisoners, as offerings to the great spirit, and the ghosts of their friends slain in war. We must do so too. The spirit of our friends will grieve if he is not burned. The white men are as cruel as we are. They killed our friends and then burned them in the house where they were killed.

*Enter a young warrior.*

*War.* The prisoner is tied to the stake. He is made black —and the fires are burning. The warriors are waiting for the order of the chiefs to begin the torture.

*Taw.* Is the prisoner afraid? Does he tremble? Or is he a man?

*War.* He is a strong man. He is not afraid. He talks to the great spirit.

*Log.* Go back young man, and tell the warriors we shall soon let them know what is to be done.

[*Exit warrior.*

*Sha.* We must not burn the prisoner. We are mistaken about these white men. They have indeed killed our friends in cold blood, but who committed this murder? The whole nation? No! Only a few bad men. All their great councils will condemn the deed. The names of their chiefs who committed those murders will be black while the world lasts. For the white men forget nothing. They write everything in their books.

*Taw.* Must we then be better than the white men?

*Sha.* Brother *Tawatwees.* Will it hurt our pride to be told that we are better than white men? Thank the great spirit, we are better than many of them. What says brother *Logan;* shall we burn the prisoner?

*Log.* A prisoner belongs to the nation. And it belongs to the chiefs to say what shall be done with him. It may be that I have done wrong and if I have I beg pardon. I have promised him his life, and *Logan* never told a lie.

*Taw.* Logan is a strong warrior; yet he grew up in the sunshine of peace; but Logan is too good. His heart is too soft. Will the spirits of his friends be satisfied if this prisoner is not burned?

*Log.* The hearts of Logan's friends were like his own, they were good, they were not hard. While living he was their chief. He is so still, and the last of his race. Their spirits are satisfied with what Logan has done. Brothers, I thank you for assisting me with the red hatchet, in taking revenge for the murder of my people. I beg the life of the prisoner. I have promised him that he should not die, and must he say with his last breath that Logan has told a lie.

*Taw.* Logan is a good man. He has promised too much to his prisoner; but he must keep his promise. Let us give him his prisoner.

*Kuhn.* Our young men will be much disappointed. They are all anxious to put the fire to the white man.

*Log.* They are young men. They will soon forget the disappointment. Logan has had revenge. He has done his duty to his people.

## SCENE III.

*Enter Queeta with her son Sheba a young warrior, and two daughters.*

*Queeta.* Fathers! Queeta's son was killed at the camp of Logan, at Yellow Creek. Queeta wants another son in his place. I will take take the prisoner in the place of my son.

*Sheba.* Sheba wants a brother. The prisoner is a strong young man. Sheba's eyes would be full of tears if he should be burned. We will hunt hard this fall. We will give fifty bucks for the prisoner.

*Young Squaws.* We want a brother. The prisoner will be a good hunter, and kill deer for us, and we will be kind to him. Good fathers! do give us the poor prisoner for a brother.

*Exeunt Queeta and her daughters.*

*All the chiefs.* Logan the prisoner is yours. Do with him as your good heart directs.

[*Exit Logan.*

*Sha.* We shall make our young warriors angry for a while; but we shall stop the blood which runs so fast from the veins of both of the white, and red men, and this is best.

*Kuhn.* Tawatwees, and Kuhn are both for blood, but Logan and Shahillas are great men. They are strong in war, and the light of their minds, is the light of the sun when he is highest in the sky. We agree, and hope it is for the best.

## SCENE IV.

*Enter Logan with the prisoner, with a belt of white wampum tied around his body.*

(*The chiefs shake hands with him, each calling him brother.*)

*Enter Queeta, with her son and daughters.*

*Log.* Mother, I give you the prisoner for a son, and you shall not pay for him. Poor mother, you, like Logan, have lost too much already! You have lost your son. The prisoner is now in his place. And now prisoner, Logan has something to tell you. When we were bringing you here, I promised you that you should not die, and I have made my promise good. Now be a man. Here is your mother, she is a good woman. Here is your brother, he is a fine young man, and here are your two sisters, they are good girls. They will be kind to you; they will not ask you to work; but you must kill meat for them. Be a good man, prisoner. Do not run away. This war cannot last always, the time may come, and that soon, when you may return to your own people, with honor, and perhaps help to stop the blood which is now running. Logan returns to the war, and you may never see him again; but whatever may be his fate, you will say that Logan has been your friend.

(*Prisoner, attempting to kneel down.*)

*Log.* Dont kneel. Stand up like a man. Logan is not the great spirit.

*Pris.* I thank you, good chiefs, for my life. I shall not run away, I shall always say that Logan has been my best friend.

*Queeta.* (*Taking the prisoner by the hand.*) My son! (*Wiping her eyes.*) Did you ever loose a brother by death?

*Pris.*   Yes mother, one of my brothers died some time ago.
*Queeta.*   Did he come to life again?
*Pris.*   No!
*Queeta.*   If he had come to life again, and you had taken him by the hand, you would know how I feel in taking you in the place of my dead son.

*Sheba.*   (*Taking the prisoner by the hand.*)   My brother! My poor brother, your feet must be very sore. (*Hands him a pair of mocassons.*) Put these mocassons on them, and then you shall go with us to our Wigwam. (*The prisoner puts the mocassons on his feet.*)

*Tawasta.*   The eldest sister. (*Taking the prisoner by the hand.*) I am your sister. You must love us, and we will be good to you.

*Neputa.*   Youngest sister. (*Taking the prisoner by the hand.*) Poor brother, he is almost naked. Here brother put this matchcoat on him. (*Hands him a matchcoat, who puts it on the prisoner.*)

[*Exeunt omnes.*

## ACT IV.

### SCENE I.—*Chilicothe.*

*War chiefs in council.*

[*Enter Warrior.*

*Sha.*   Warrior, where have you been?

*War.*   I am one of the spies sent by the *Tawatwees* to watch the tracks of the white men, I have been out one moon.

*Sha.*   And what have you seen brother?

*War.*   Too much. They are coming upon us as thick as grasshoppers. Capt. Dunmore is coming up the Hockhocking, and Capt. Lewis lower down. They intend meeting in this town.

*Sha.* How do you know that?

*War.* One dark night I got close to two of their men, who watch on the outside of the camp, and I heard them say that they would have fine fun, and plenty to eat in Chilicothe in a few days, and the great captain and their warriors would shake hands there.

*Sha.* Are you sure of this, warrior? Do you understand their talk?

*War.* Yes I do. Too much.

[*Exit warrior.*

*Kuhn.* The dark clouds are coming close to us. What shall we do brothers? Shall we fight; or make peace with the long knives? We must do something very soon.

*Taw.* It may be that the great spirit is angry with us, because we drink too much of the strong water made by the white men, and because we did not burn Logan's prisoner. Let us make him an offering. (*He clears away every thing from around the council fire, after which he and the other chiefs draw each an handfull of tobacco from their pouches, and throw it into the fire.*)

*Taw.* O! Great Spirit! We have made you an offering of tobacco. Now hear us, your red children. The white men are coming to kill us, and our squaws and children. Oh! Great Spirit, make these white men sick with the fever, that there may be a great many new graves about all their camps, so their hearts may be made weak. Make all the deer and turkies go away from about them, that they may become hungry and go home. O! Great Spirit, make the two great captains get mad, quarrel, and fight with one another and go way from us. O! Great Spirit, make the hearts, and hands of your red children strong to fight these long knives, and kill and drive them away from our country.

*Brothers*, we must remove our squaws and children to Lower

Sanduskey, out of the way of the long knives, or they will kill them all. Then me must fight them and drive them away if we can.

*Sha.* Brothers, it is too late. The snow will soon come. If we take away our squaws and children they will starve; for the white men will destroy all our corn. We cannot fight. We have too little powder and lead. We must make peace.

*Kuhn.* Will they make peace with us? I think they are too angry. They want to kill us all, and take all our land. We must fight to the last.

*Sha.* The long knives from Kenhawa are very angry, and would kill all our squaws and children as well as ourselves, if they could; but the great captain Dunmore, and his men are not as bad. They will make peace with us.

*Kuhn.* How do you know that?

*Sha.* It may be that I have done wrong. I have sent a messenger to Capt. Dunmore to ask him if he would make peace. He says he will. His messenger with a white flag will be here presently. We must make peace with Capt. Dunmore, before the long knives from Kenhawa join them, Capt. Dunmore is not angry; but the long knives are very angry.

*Log.* This war was made for Logan, and he had revenge for the death of all his people; but he is sorry that so many of our warriors have been killed by the long knives. Brothers you suffered too much for Logan; he is but one man.

*Kuhn.* Brother, we have not done too much for you. We are all one, and we must help all our brothers.

## SCENE II.

*Enter a messenger from the camp of Dunmore, with a roll of paper in his hand.*

*Mes.* Your brother, Capt. Dunmore, sends me to the chiefs with this white flag.
(*To Logan.*) *Captain Logan, I am glad to see you.*
*Log.* (*angrily.*) May be so.
(*To the Interpreter,*) stand by me, (*reads.*)
The Earl of Dunmore, Governor of the province of Virginia, makes known to the chiefs of the nations, now unhappily confederated in hostility, against the good subjects of his majesty the king of England, that, deprecating on his part, the bloodshed and miseries of war, he is desirous of entering into an honorable and permanent peace, with the Indian nations, now at war, and will gladly receive all the chiefs at camp Charlotte tomorrow at noon, should it be their wish to enter into a treaty of peace.

[*Exit messenger.*

## SCENE III.

*Enter a young warrior.*

*Kuhn.* What news have you?
*War.* Captain Lewis and his long knives are coming up the Scioto, like a whirlwind. They will be here the day after tomorrow, to kill us all, if they can. I heard their watchmen on the outside of the camp say so. They are very angry, because so many of their men were killed at the Kenhawa.

*Taw.* Did you hear them say any thing about Capt. Dunmore?

*War.* Yes. I heard them say that Capt. Dunmore is the biggest captain. They are afraid that he will make peace with the Indians, before they can get to Chilicothe. They want to get here first and kill all the Indians, before Capt. Dunmore makes peace.

[*Exit warrior.*

*Kuhn.* What shall we do? Shall we take our squaws and children away from the long knives? They will kill them all if they can.

*Sha.* We will not send our squaws and children away yet. We must send a messenger to the big Capt. Dunmore with the talk of the warriors, and he will send one of his captains to tell Capt. Lewis to stop; if he dont do so we will move off our squaws and children as fast as we can, and then sell our wigwams and corn to the long knives, for as many of them as we can kill.

*Taw.* Call the warrior, and give him the white flag, to go to the big Capt. Dunmore.

*Enter warrior.*

*Sha.* (*Hands him a white handkerchief on a stick.*) Take this to the big Capt. Dunmore, and give him the same talk which you have given us.

[*Exit warrior.*

*Sha.* Who shall go to the camp of Capt. Dunmore tomorrow? We must make peace, as soon as we can; or we shall have bad times.

*Taw.* I am afraid of these white men. They are all liars. They want to get us into their camp, and then kill us all, like they did our friends at Yellow creek. May be, we had better move off first, and then make peace if we can.

*Kuhn.* There is no time to be lost. The long knives are close to us, and we have a great many squaws, and children, and wounded men to take care of. Our people must begin to pack up to go away.

*Sha.* They may do so, if they choose; but if they do so, it must not be told. It would make Capt. Dunmore very angry, if he should be told of our preparing to go away. He would say that we dont believe what he says. We must appear to believe these white men; altho' we know them to be very great liars.

*Log.* There is no danger. Capt. Dunmore will make peace with us. The dark clouds are coming from the other side of the great water where Capt. Dunmore lives. The great chief of the white men is getting very angry with his children here, because they dont give him money enough. He will soon lift the red hatchet against them. Logan has had revenge for the death of his friends. He has killed many. The rest he leaves to the white men themselves. They will save Logan the trouble of killing any more of them. They will cut each others throats very soon. The great chief over the great water will want the red men to join him. Capt. Dunmore knows all this. He will make peace. He came here to save us from the long knives.

*Kuhn.* We must all go to the camp of the great captain tomorrow.

*Log.* Go brothers, with all our warriors; but Logan will not go. Logan will never look in the face of a white man, with the words of peace in his mouth. Logan consents to bury the red hatchet for the sake of his brothers; who have already suffered too much for him. Here interpreter take this talk to Capt. Dunmore.

(*Reads the speech from a belt of white wampum, and then hands it to the interpreter.*)

"I appeal to any white man to say, if ever he entered Logan's cabin hungry, and he gave him not meat: if ever he came cold and naked, and he clothed him not. During the course of the last long and bloody war Logan remained idle in his cabin, an advocate for peace. Such was my love for the whites, that my country-men pointed as they passed, and said, 'Logan is the friend of the white men.' I had even thought to have lived with you, but for the injuries of one man. Colonel Cresap, the last spring, in cold blood, and unprovoked, murdered all the relations of Logan, not even sparing my women and children. There runs not a drop of my blood in the veins of any living creature. This called on me for revenge. I have sought it. I have killed many: I have fully glutted my vengeance: for my country I rejoice at the beams of peace. But do not harbour a thought that mine is the joy of fear. Logan never felt fear. He will not turn on his heel to save his life. Who is there to mourn for Logan?—Not one."

*(Exeunt omnes.*

# A DIALOGUE

BETWEEN

A DANDY AND A BACK-WOODS-MAN.

# PREFACE.

The following dialogue was composed at the request of the students of the Buffaloe Seminary and recited at their last exhibition. It was well received by the audience. Since then it has received some attention in different parts of the country and been recited in different schools and Thespian Societies. The author has therefore thought proper to republish it under his own name.

Some expressions in this dialogue may appear rough and uncouth, and a few of them objectionable on another ground. Let the blame, if any, rest where it ought; it is not the fault of the author, more than it was that of Shakespeare that "the age in which he lived was not an age of delicacy." Like others in the dramatic personification, the author has used the proverbs, idiom, and phraseology of those people whose manners he intended to represent.

If some expressions in the dialogue should excite the blush and blame of prudery, no matter. The historian like the connoisseur in painting and statuary, is best pleased with a portrait faithful to the features and figure of its original. This little dialogue is such. The state of society which it describes is precisely such as existed at the period of time alluded to. Even the facts stated by "the Back-woods-man" are historical. Its language that which was in current use among our first settlers.

From a portrait of the manners of former times, we have it in our power to make a contrast of two widely different states of society, which results in a conclusion, in favor of the present, which cannot fail to be highly gratifying to every lover of the physical, moral, and religious happiness of man.

WELLSBURGH, *September* the 2 1823.

# A DIALOGUE

## BETWEEN A DANDY AND A BACK-WOODS-MAN.

The following original dialogue, was first acted at the last exhibition at the Buffaloe Seminary, with great applause—by Mr. Samuel Mitchel, in the character of the Back-woods-man, and Mr. John Andrews, in that of the Dandy.

The curtain rises and presents the Back-woods-man in an hunting shirt, a shot-pouch, with his powderhorn on his right side, with his feet and legs, dressed, of course, in leggins and mockasons. A Spruce little Dandy in the dress of his order approaches him. The dialogue then begins.

*Dandy.* Good morning sir. I am glad to see you; I have often heard and read of the Back-woods-men: and supposing, from your dress you are one of them, I should like to have a little conversation with you, concerning the first settlement of this country, and your wars with the Indians.

*Back-woods-man.*—With all my heart.

*Dan.* I have no doubt your tales of former times are highly interesting and entertaining, and of course worthy of remembrance.

*Back.* For the matter of that, I cannot say much in their favor. I have no larnin, an I never was much of a hand at tellin tales; howenever, I will do with you as I have often seed them do in the Court, in West Liberty, I will answer such questons as you will ax me.

*Dan.* What time did you come to this country?

*Back.* In the year 1773, the summer before Dunmore's war,

my father came over the mountins, and settled in this part of the country. I was then a thumpin chunk of a boy, may be ten or a dozen years old.

*Dan.* What was the external appearance of the country at at your first recollection of it?

*Back.* Why, Sir, the tarnal appearance of the country was, that it was all wild woods, and full of deers, and bears, and turkies, and rattlesnakes—and in the summer time, the weeds was so high, that you could track a man on horseback, at full galop.

*Dan.* I suppose, Sir, you had then but few of the comforts of civilized life.

*Back.* Why, we was not very fine to be sure, but we was civil enough; for the war which placed our night caps in danger every day, made us very lovin to one another; one man then was worth as much as twenty is now; but if you mean fine things about house, and stores, and mills, and meeting houses, and big roads, we had no such things; or if you mean squires, and preachers, and lawyers, and judges, and sheriffs, we had no such cattle among us for many years.

*Dan.* How could society exist in such circumstances? What was your diet?

*Back.* We subsisted as well as we could. Our vittals was venzon, bear meat, wild turkies, and arter we got to raisin corn we had plenty of mush and milk and hog and homony.

*Dan.* And pray, old gentleman, what was the furniture of your houses in those early times?

*Back.* The furniture of our cabbins was trenches, woodin bowls, gourds, and hard shelled squashes, and some times a few old pewter plates, and tin cups.

*Dan.* But tell me, how did you procure those indispensable necessaries without which society cannot subsist?

*Back.* O! Don't you talk so high flowin. What do you mean by spensable necessaries?

*Dan.* I mean salt, iron, steel, and such like things.

*Back.* O! I understand you now; I will tell you all about that. We gathered all the deer skins, and bear skins, and fur that we could get through the year, and every fall the neighbors would join the gither and rig up a parcel of our horses aud packsaddles, and load them with oats and corn, and leave some at Red Stone, Tomleson's, Oldtown, Hagerstown, and Fredericktown, to feed the horses on the return ; our wallets were filled with cakes and good jirk. When we got to Baltimore we sold our skins and fur for iron, steel, and salt and powder and lead, and some tin cups, and if a little stranger or a wedding was shortly expected in one of the families, a half a pound of bohea tea was sometimes fetched out for the frolic. This was drunk out of tin cups, if we happened to have them, if not, we drunk it out of noggins or bowls.

I must tell you a bit of a joke to let you know how little we knowed about things on tother side of the mountins. Sometime after the country had been settled, a parcel of us undertook to take a drove of beeves to Baltimore; at a sartin place in the mountins, where we staid all night, our landlord and his hired man stole two of our bells. The drove had not gone far in the mornin before the bells was missed; some of our men went back, made search, got the bells and hung them round the necks of the laddies and marched them before them till they overtook the drove; a jury was held, and they was condemned to take so many lashes from each drovyer. They were stript to the buff, and tied up to the trees. When the drovyer that owned one of the bells got the hickory in his hand, now? says he, you infernal scoundrel I'll work your jacket nineteen to a dozen. Only what a pityful figure I should have made parading the streets of Baltimore without a bell on my horse.

*Dan.* What was your education in those days?

*Back.* I will tell you what my larnin was. Soon arter I had larn'd to speak, I larned to mock every bird, and beast in the woods; I could bleat like a fawn; kwock like a turkey; oohoo like an owl; and howl like a wolf, with the face of clay—next I larned to shoot the bow and arrow, throw the tomhok, and handle the rifle; and I finished by runin, jumpin, and wraslin, and depend upon it, it took a fellow of spunk to measure the ground with my back.

*Dan.* I suppose you must have been an excellent marksman?

*Back.* Let me alone for that, I could have hit a midge's eye fifty yards, if I could have seed it. A squirrels head on the top of a tree was a sure mark for me; if I once drew sight on it, I was sure to open his brain pan, and make him hunt for the ground the shortest way he could find it. By the time I was fourteen years of age, I was made a soldier in the fort, and had all my war apparatusses, and a port hole to defend: I was then of more value than I am now, every man, woman, and child considered me as one of their protectors, but now I am getting old and out of date.

*Dan.* Father! I hope not. But I must say yours was a strange state of society; every man was a hunter, a soldier, or if you please, a 'sharp shooter' and a farmer.

*Back.* Aye, indeed, it was all that.

*Dan.* I have read that the state of society may be ascertained by certain criteria such as marriage ceremonies, songs, stories and so on. Will you be so good as to give me an account of one of your marriages.

*Back.* Surely I will. In some places we had some old man

who said he had been a minister or squire, or an elder who said some kind of a ceremony for a marriage, and it did very well, they lived together as well arterwards as our people do now.

*Dan.* Relate, if you please, the whole process of a wedding.

*Back.* A weddin made a great rumpuss in a neighborhood every body that was not ax'd was mad as a wet hen, so that there was often a great deal of fun, and a great deal of mischief at a weddin.

In the mornin of the marriage day, the company gathered at the house of the groom, and tuck their march, two and two, boys and gals, to go to the bride's house. When they got about half way, two men would single out to run for the bottle, and such a race you never saw, thro' brush, over logs, up hill and down dale, till they come to the bride's house. He that got first to the bride's house, got black betty, which was the name they called the bottle; back he run as if old nick were arter him till he met the company. He was the clever fellow. The company stopt, and every boy and gal, old and young, big and little, must kiss black betty; that is to take a good slug of dram. But it often happened that the neighbors that was not ax'd, took it into their heads to make mischief, they would fall tree tops, and tie grape vines a cross the road, and sometimes plant themselves behind logs and brushes, with their guns, and fire them off so as to cover the whole company with smoke, and then such jumpin of hosses, and squallin of the gals, you never heard; sometimes the hosses would make their riders hunt for the ground, and if an elbow or shoulder was out of joint, no matter, it was soon well again. In the night, the people that was not ax'd, would cut off the mains and tails of the hosses belonging to the weddin company.

I once saw a couple of horns set up on two poles, one on

each side of the road, where a weddin company had to pass. Do you know the meanin of that? If you don't they did, and it had like to played the deal and turned up Jack.*

*Dan.* I should like to hear something of their toasts and healths on these occasions.

*Back.* They had no toast that I know of but what was made of bread, and not much of that nather, for in them days we had but little bread beside jonnycake and pone, and if you wouldn't cut that you might let it alone. When a man wanted to drink a health at a weddin, he would call out, where is black betty? I want to kiss her sweet lips. When he got the bottle he would say, 'here's to the company, not forgetting myself; and here's to the bride and groom—thumpin luck and big children.

*Dan.* Had they any other kinds of amusements but such as you have mentioned?

*Back.* O yes! They danced jigs and reels like all the world, and when they got tired, some would call a halt for a story or a song. Then would come a story about Jack and the jiant, in which the jiant was sure to come out of the little end of the horn; when this is done, some pretty gal would sing a good love song about murder, and so on they went, sometimes three or four days, may be a whole week. It was a high frolic, you may depend on it. Your wedners are as still as mice—I dont like it; marriage commonly comes but once in a body's life and there ought to be some fun about it. But new lords have new laws.

*Dan.* I perceive sir, that the ladies in your days of old, were not so well polished as they are now; they had no rings, ruffles, and leghorns.

*Back.* Some few of them got some brass rings from their mothers, or grand mothers, but they was not thought the better

---

* This was frequently done when the chastity of the bride was suspected.

# A DIALOGUE.

for wearing them; as for ruffles, they had not much to make them of; as for leghorns, I cant say much about them—legs to be sure they had, but I don't know that any of them had horns.

*Dan.* I perceive from all you have said Mr. Back-woodsman, that you must have been in a deplorable condition—your country a willderness; your habitations wretched hovels, or cabbins; your furniture gourds, your marriages scenes of riot and obscenity: No places of worship; no schools, courts, nor civil government of any sort; a continual warfare with the Indians. No comforts; no elegancies for the body, and no means of improvement for the mind—Heavens! What a condition of human society! Was this country a Tartary or a Siberia? Surely, Sir, you must have been neither more nor less than a set of semi barbarians!

(*At this last expression, the Backwoodsman darts a look of indignation at the dandy.*)

*Back.* Young Buck! you have called me Back-woods-man, and I confessed my name and I have answered all the questions you have ax'd me; now pray, who are you? Some time ago my daughter Betsy, showed me a picture in Mr. Berry's paper, and she said it was a thing called a Dandy, and you hemlook very much like it, with your bell crowned hat. How many capes have you got on your coat? Look at trumpet muzzled trowsers there? What makes your waist so slim? You must have cords around you to pull up the ribs, and squeeze in the breadbasket, and must I suffer such a little finikin, puny pinched up thing, to call me and the rest of the first settlers of this country, simple barbarians? Young thing, I am old to be sure, but there is oil enough in my bones for you yet.

(*The Backwoodsman draws his fist, hits the Dandy in the face, who falls at length on the floor, his cane and hat fall at some distance from him.*)

*Dan.* Murder! help! help! For God's sake deliver me! (*Several come running to his assistance.*)
*Back.* Stop young men, I shall not strike him any more. Let him get up himself, I have not hurt him much, I'm sure. Get up pigmy.
(*The Dandy endeavours to rise, but is unable on account of his corslets.*)
*Back.* What's the matter with him? His whole body is as stiff as a stake. Give me your hand. (*He helps him up, and politely hands him his hat and cane.*)
*Dan.* For what reason did you strike me? It was not my intention to give you any offense; you must have mistaken the meaning of what I said.
*Back.* No matter young man I go off half cocked sometimes; thats all. And now I'll tell you a piece of my mind—A Backwoods-man is a queer sort of a fellow; he never gives an affront, and he never takes one; if you call him a rogue, a liar, or a simple barbarian, he will be sure to knock you down, or try for it. If he's not a man of larnin, he has plain good sense. If his dress is not fine, his inside works are good and his heart is sound. If he is not rich or great, he knows that he is a father of his country. Yes, young man, instead of that pretty little stick, I have had to handle the rifle and the tomahoc. Instead of a bell crowned hat, I have had to score the woods with an old bit of a hankerchy on my head, in scoutin arter Ingins. Instead of such a smelling bottle as you hold to your nose, I have had to smell gunpowder. The little land I own has been dearly purchased by the blood of my relations! You little dandies, and other big folks may freely enjoy the fruits of our hardships; you may feast, where we had to starve; you may frolic, where we had to fight; but at the peril of all of you, give the Back-woods-man, none of your slack jaw.

The patrons of, "The notes on the settlement, and wars of the western country." Are informed that the work only awaits the fulfilment of a contract for paper, rendered impracticable for some time past, by the want of water in the stream on which the mill is situated.

The author is thankful to those gentlemen who have returned the subscriptions sent to them; and hopes those who have not done so, will return theirs with all convenient despatch.

WELLSBURGH, *September* the 13 1823.

# APPENDIX.

### I.—LOGAN—THE MURDER OF HIS FAMILY—HIS REVENGE.

*We extract the following account of Logan from "Red Men of the Ohio Valley," by J. R. Dodge, p. 132.*

Logan, whose name has been rendered immortal by his touchingly eloquent speech to Lord Dunmore, was a son of Skikellimus, a head chief of the Iroquois living on the Susquehanna, a disciple of the Moravian missionaries of Count Zinzendorf, whom the old chief had entertained on his visit to Shamokin, Pennsylvania, in 1742. When he appeared as a candidate for baptism, the missionaries hesitated on account of his having been baptized previously by a Catholic priest in Canada—upon which he destroyed a small idol which he always wore about his neck. He was a man of influence and integrity. Skikellimus had a high regard for James Logan, Secretary of the Province of Pennsylvania, and named his son for him. The early life of Logan was spent in Pennsylvania, where he acquired an enviable character for kindness and amiability. His personal appearance was commanding. David Zeisberger, the Moravian friend of his father, speaks of him as a man of quick comprehension and good judgment.

Hon. R. P. Maclay gives an anecdote in illustration, which has its scene in Mifflin county, at the Big Spring, four miles west of Logan's Spring, where Judge Brown, the first settler of the Kishacoquillas Valley, was surprised by the Indian Logan.

## APPENDIX.

"The first time I saw the spring," said the old gentleman[*] to a brother of the narrator of this anecdote, "my brother, James Reed and myself, had wandered out of the valley in search of land, and finding it good, were looking about for springs. About a mile from this we started a bear, and separated to get a shot at him. I was traveling along, looking about on the rising ground for the bear, when I came suddenly upon the spring, and being dry, and more rejoiced to find so fine a spring than to have killed a dozen bears, I set my rifle against a bush and rushed down the bank, and laid down to drink. Upon putting my head down, I saw reflected in the water, on the opposite side, the shadow of a tall Indian. I sprang to my rifle, when the Indian gave a yell, whether for peace or war I was not just then sufficiently master of my faculties to determine; but upon my seizing my rifle and facing him, he knocked up the pan of his gun, threw out the priming, and extended his open palm to me in token of friendship. After putting down our guns, we again met at the spring and shook hands. This was Logan—the best specimen of humanity I ever met with, either *white* or *red*. He could speak a little English, and told me there was another white hunter a little way down the stream, and offered to guide me to his camp. There I first met your father. We remained together in the valley a week, looking for springs and selecting lands, and laid the foundation of a friendship which never had the slightest interruption.

"We visited the camp at Logan's Spring, and your father and he shot at a mark for a dollar a shot. Logan lost four or five rounds, and acknowledged himself beaten. When we were about to leave him he went into his hut and brought out as many deerskins as he had lost dollars, and handed them to Mr. Maclay, who refused to take them, alleging that we had been his guests, and

---

[*] Judge Brown.

did not come to rob him; that the shooting had been only a trial of skill, and the bet merely nominal. Logan drew himself up with great dignity, and said, 'Me bet to make you shoot your best—me gentleman, and me take your dollar if me beat.' So he was obliged to take the skins, or affront our friend, whose nice sense of honor would not permit him to receive even a horn of powder in return."

Mrs. Norris, a daughter of the old judge, living near the spring, is authority for further incidents in the life of this aboriginal celebrity.

Logan supported his family by killing deer, dressing the skins, and selling them to the whites. He had sold quite a parcel to one De Yong, a tailor, who lived in Ferguson's Valley, below the gap. Tailors in those days dealt extensively in buckskin breaches. Logan received his pay, according to stipulation, in wheat. The wheat, on being taken to the mill, was found so worthless that the miller refused to grind it. Logan was much chagrined, and attempted in vain to obtain redress from the tailor. He then took the matter before his friend Brown, then a magistrate; and on the judge's questioning him as to the character of the wheat and what was in it, Logan sought in vain to find words to express the precise nature of the article with which the wheat was adulterated, but said that it resembled in appearance the wheat itself. "It must have been *cheat*," said the judge. "Yoh," said Logan, "that very good name for him." A decision was awarded in Logan's favor, and a writ given to Logan to hand to the constable, which, he was told, would bring him the money for his skins. But the untutored Indian—too uncivilized to be dishonest—could not understand by what magic this little paper would force the tailor against his will to pay for the skins. The judge took down his own commission, with the arms of the king upon it, and explained to him the first principles and operations of civil law. "Law good," said Logan, "make rogues pay." But how much more simple and effective was the law which the Great Spirit had impressed upon his heart—*to do as he would be done by!*

When a sister of Mrs. Norris (afterwards Mrs. General Potter) was just beginning to learn to walk, her mother happened to express her regret that she could not get her a pair of shoes to give more firmness to her step. Logan stood by, but said nothing. He soon after asked Mrs. Brown to let the little girl go up and spend the day at his cabin. The cautious heart of the mother was alarmed at such a proposition; but she knew the delicacy of an Indian's feelings—and she knew Logan, too—and with a secret reluctance, but apparent cheerfulness, she complied with his request. The hours of the day wore slowly away, and it was nearly night, when her little one had not returned. But just as the sun was going down, the trusty chief was seen coming down the path with his charge; and in a moment more the little one trotted into its mother's arms, proudly exhibiting a beautiful pair of moccasins on her little feet, the product of Logan's skill.

During the old French war, Logan lived in Pennsylvania, a firm friend of the whites. After his removal to the Indian town which bore his name, situated on the west side of the Ohio River, a little above Cross Creeks, seventy-five miles below Pittsburg, his revenge was aroused by the murder of his family, near the mouth of Yellow Creek, in what is now Jefferson County.

Injustice seems to have been done to the memory of Colonel Cresap, in the popular mind, by attributing to him this cruel and impolitic transaction. Logan, in his famous speech, alludes to him as the murderer of his family. As good authority as that of George Rogers Clark entirely exonerates him from all connection with the affair. It seems that Dr. John Conolly, a nephew

*APPENDIX.*

of George Croghan, a resident of Virginia, sought to establish the exclusive authority of that State over Fort Pitt and vicinity. He issued a proclamation for a gathering for military organization at Redstone, now Brownsville, on the 24th and 25th of January, 1774, but was arrested before the time appointed by Arthur St. Clair, who represented the Pennsylvania proprietors. On his release, he came to Pittsburg, in March, and in the name and under authority of Lord Dunmore, he commenced building the fort, which he called Fort Dunmore. His course tended palpably to precipitate a war with the Indians, and seemed to be shaped purposely to accomplish that end. He wrote inflammatory letters to Virginians, accusing the Indians of stealing horses from the settlements, and committing other depredations.

An alarm spread through the border, occasioned by the killing of a white man near Wheeling by a band of Cherokees. A party of Virginia surveyors and explorers, under the lead of Captain Cresap, repaired at once to Wheeling. Clark was one of this party. At this time a letter was received from Conolly, requesting them to remain in position a few days; and soon after, another, informing him that war was inevitable; that the country should be covered with scouts, and the inhabitants should fortify themselves. In this exigency, a council of settlers and Indian traders was called, and war was formally declared. During the same evening two scalps were brought in, probably those of friendly Indians, who had been sent by the trader, William Butler, to look after the cargo of the canoe attacked by the Cherokees. Ebenezer Zane opposed the killing of these Indians without avail. The party accused, upon being questioned about them, coolly replied that they had fallen overboard from the boat into the river.

The day following this war declaration, canoes of Indians were seen on the river, screening themselves from view under cover of an island.  They were chased fifteen miles, engaged in battle, in which a few were wounded on both sides, and one Indian taken prisoner.  Ammunition and other warlike stores were found in their canoes.  It was agreed that the party should march the next day to the attack of Logan's camp, some thirty miles up the river.  The expedition was entered upon; and when within five miles of the camp, the impropriety of executing the enterprise was urged by Cresap himself, on the ground of its injustice, as it was generally agreed that these Indians were friendly.  The party willingly returned, disgusted with the undertaking—starting the same evening in the direction of the Redstone.

A few days after this, occurred the Yellow Creek tragedy.  On the Virginia side, at a settlement of a man named Baker, a party of thirty-two whites was gathered under the lead of Captain Daniel Greathouse.  From an Indian encampment upon the other side, came a party of five men, bringing with them one woman and her infant child.  Three of the men were plied with rum till they were drunk; the other two and the woman, refusing to drink, were shot down, while the drunken Indians were tomahawked.  The little pappoose was saved, at the intercession of the mother, who reminded them that the little half-breed was akin to themselves.  The Indians, hearing the firing over the river, sent two men to make inquiries about it, who were shot down as they leaped from their canoes upon the beach.  A larger deputation was received in the same way, many of them being killed, and the remainder compelled to retire.  The murdered Indians were scalped.  Shots were exchanged across the river without effect.  None of the whites were even wounded.  The survivors fled down the river.  Thus resulted this treacherous, cowardly and disgraceful affair, in which three of the nearest relatives of Logan, probably his brother and a sister, were inhumanly butchered.

This aroused the tiger in that amiable chieftain, and he swore that the tomahawk should drink the blood of the white man, till its vengeance should be appeased with a tenfold expiation. His oath was kept, and more than thirty are said to have fallen during the summer of 1774, by the hand of Logan.

Logan had been a persistent friend of the whites, and had just persuaded to peace an Indian council, declaring that the "Long Knives," or Virginians, would come like trees in the woods, and drive them from their lands, unless the hatchet was laid down. His counsel prevailed, and he was rewarded for his fidelity by the murder of his family in cold blood.

Some time was yet spent in negotiations with the Ohio Indians. The Delawares were inclined for peace; the Senecas and Shawnees urged them to take up the hatchet, taunted them, calling them *Shwonnocks*, or whites, greatly to the exasperation of the young Delawares. Dr. Conolly still sought to stir up war, and it is said intercepted their Shawnee guides on a return from an escort of whites, wounding one, even after they had once been saved from his clutches by his uncle, George Croghan. War was inevitable; and before the month of August, the Shawnees, and Senecas or Mingoes, recruited by a few Delawares and Cherokees, were in the field.

Logan, with a band of eight chosen warriors, boldly penetrated the white settlements at the head waters of the Monongahela, took many scalps, captured several prisoners, and led them off in safety, eluding all pursuit, and defying all attempts at capture.

"One of the incidents attending this incursion deserves to be mentioned, as illustrating the character of Logan. While hovering, with his followers, around the skirts of a thick settlement, he suddenly came within view of a small field, recently cleared, in which three men were pulling flax. Causing the greater part of his men to remain where they were, Logan, together with two others, crept up within long shot of the white men and fired. One man fell dead, the remaining two attempted to escape. The elder of the fugitives, (Hellew,) was quickly overtaken and made prisoner by Logan's associates, while Logan himself, having thrown down his rifle, pressed forward alone in pursuit of the younger of the white men, whose name was Robinson. The contest was keen for several hundred yards, but Robinson, unluckily, looking around, in order to have a view of his pursuer, ran against a tree with such violence as completely to stun him, and render him insensible for several minutes.

Upon recovering, he found himself bound, and lying upon his back, while Logan sat by his side, with unmoved gravity, awaiting his recovery. He was then compelled to accompany them in their further attempts upon the settlements, and in the course of a few days, was marched off with great rapidity for their villages in Ohio. During the march, Logan remained silent and melancholy, probably brooding over the total destruction of his family. The prisoners, however, were treated kindly, until they arrived at an Indian village upon the Muskingum. When within a mile of the town, Logan became more animated, and uttered the "scalp hallo" several times, in the most terrible tones. The never failing scene of insult and torture then began. Crowds flocked out to meet them, and a line was formed for the gauntlet.

Logan took no share in the cruel game, but did not attempt to repress it. He, however, gave Robinson, whom he regarded as his own prisoner, some directions as to the best means of reaching the council house in safety, and displayed some anxiety for his safe arrival, while poor Hellew was left in total ignorance, and permitted to struggle forward as best he could. Robinson, under the patronage of Logan, escaped with a few slight bruises, but

Hellew, not knowing where to run, was dreadfully mangled, and would probably have been killed upon the spot, had not Robinson (not without great risk on his own part) seized him by the hand and dragged him into the council house.

On the following morning, a council was called in order to determine their fate, in which Logan held a conspicuous superiority over all who were assembled. Hellew's destiny came first under discussion, and was quickly decided by an almost unanimous vote of adoption. Robinson's was most difficult to determine. A majority of the council (partly influenced by a natural thirst for vengeance upon at least *one* object, partly, perhaps, by a lurking jealousy of the most imposing superiority of Logan's character,) were obstinately bent upon putting him to death. Logan spoke for nearly an hour upon the question; and if Robinson is to be believed, with an energy, copiousness, and dignity, which would not have disgraced Henry himself. He appeared at at no loss for either words or ideas; his tones were deep and musical, and were heard by the assembly with the silence of death. All, however, was vain. Robinson was condemned, and within an hour afterward, was fastened to the stake. Logan stood apart from the crowd with his arms folded, and his eyes fixed upon the scene with an air of stern displeasure.

When the fire was about to be applied, he suddenly strode into the circle, pushing aside those who stood in the way, and advancing straight up to the stake, cut the cords with his tomahawk, and taking the prisoner by the hand, led him with a determined air to his own wigwam. The action was so totally unexpected, and the air of the chief so determined, that he had reached the door of his wigwam before any one ventured to interfere. Much dissatisfaction was then expressed, and threatening symptoms of a tumult appeared; but so deeply rooted was his authority, that in a few hours all was quiet, and Robinson, without opposition, was permitted to enter an Indian family. He remained with Logan until the treaty of Fort Pitt, in the autumn of the ensuing year, when he returned to Virginia. He ever retained the most unbounded admiration for Logan, and repeatedly declared that his countenance, when speaking, was the most striking, varied, and impressive, that he ever beheld. An when it is recollected that he had often heard Lee and Henry, in all their glory, the compliment must be regarded as a very high one."[*]

Afterward, at the dictation of Logan, with some ink made with gunpowder, the following letter was written, and afterward found tied to a war-club in a house, on the north fork of Helston Creek, of a family that had been cut off by the Indians:

"CAPTAIN CRESAP:—What did you kill my people on Yellow Creek for? The white people killed my kin at Conestoga, a great while ago, and I thought nothing of that. But you killed my kin again, on Yellow Creek, and took my cousin prisoner. Then I thought I must kill too, and I have been three times to war since; but the Indians are not angry—only myself.
                                    CAPTAIN JOHN LOGAN."

The Long Knives, as the Virginians were called, now made a foray upon the Ohio territory, led by Colonel McDonald, who descended the great river to the mouth of Captina Creek, and thence pushed his way to the village of Wapatomica, on the Muskingum, destroying several villages on the way, and returning safely with three chiefs as prisoners. In August, the governor of Virginia raised three entire regiments west of the Blue Ridge, and placed General Andrew Lewis in command; at the same time an equal force, under command of Lord Dunmore, marched to form a junction with Lewis at the mouth of the Great Kanawha.

---

[*] *From Appendix to "Western Adventure," by John A. McClung, p. 278.*

## APPENDIX. 63

At the site of Lewisburg, Va., Lewis was joined by an independent regiment of Virginia volunteers, under command of Colonel John Fields, a brave and able officer. With forces now augmented to eleven hundred men, the commander awaited the coming of Col. Christian, with another regiment. After waiting a few days, without hearing any tidings from him, the order was given to march to the place of rendezvous. Dunmore had not yet arrived. At length a dispatch was received, telling Lewis that he had changed his plan, and designed to march at once upon the Scioto villages, whither Lewis was directed to repair. Disappointed at this change of route, he yet prepared to obey his superior, and promptly commenced preparations for crossing the Ohio. On the morning of October 10th, two men were fired upon while scouting a mile or more from the camp. One was killed; the other gained the camp, and gave notice of the presence of a body of Indians. Colonel Charles Lewis, with one hundred and fifty Augusta troops, was posted to the right, and Colonel Fleming, with one hundred and fifty Botetourt, Bedford and Fincastle troops, were ordered to the bank of the Ohio on the left. Colonel Lewis had marched scarcely a half mile, when, about sunrise, he received the attack of a large body of hostile Indians, and at the same time Fleming was engaged on the left. The attack was made with savage impetuosity, and repelled with heroic bravery. Soon both commandants fell mortally wounded, and the right wing was forced to yield, until reinforced by eight companies under command of Col. Fields. The Indians were now compelled to give away. Thus the battle raged till noon, and was continued, at intervals during the day. Under cover of the night the Indians retired, having made excellent use of the advantages enjoyed by their slow retreat, the close underwood and steep banks, in carrying off their wounded and throwing their dead into the Ohio. The loss of the whites was severe—fifty-two men killed, half the commissioned officers, and nearly two hundred wounded; the Indians' loss is unknown—thirty-three were found upon the field, and many of the dead were thrown into the river. The probabilities are that the loss was pretty nearly equal. The Indian force engaged was about eleven hundred. Thus closed the ghastly scenes of the battle of Point Pleasant, one of the most sanguinary of Indian conflicts in the Valley of the Ohio. Logan, Cornstalk, Ellinipsico, Red Hawk, and other chiefs of note, are said to have been present. Cornstalk's voice rung high above the din of battle—"Be strong! Be strong!" When a warrior manifested symptoms of fright, he is said to have buried his hatchet in his brain as cooly as if he had been a pale face.

Lord Dunmore, with his division, numbering as many as that of General Lewis, passed the mountains at the Potomac Gap, and crossed the Ohio above Wheeling. A talk was had with the Senecas and Delawares on the 6th of October. Passing down the river to the mouth of the Hockhocking, a halt was made and Fort Gower was erected. At this point—twenty-eight miles above Point Pleasant—during the fight, the roar of the musketry was distinctly heard by placing the ear upon the ground. Dunmore proceeded to the present site of Logan, Hocking county, and thence west to the left bank of Sippo Creek, seven miles southeast of Circleville. This encampment was named Camp Charlotte.

A messenger was sent hence to intercept General Lewis. Fired with zeal for signal victory over the Red Men, and smarting under the loss of his brother, he felt little inclination to heed the command of Dunmore, but pressed to Congo Creek, within striking distance of the Indian towns of Pickaway, and near to Old Chillicothe, the site of the present village of Westfall. The infuriated Virginians could scarcely be restrained; they ventured to charge the royal governor with attempting to form an alliance with the Indian tribes for the benefit of Great Britain in the approaching revolutionary struggle. Dunmore went to enforce his orders in person, and drew his sword on General Lewis, threatening him with instant death if he persisted in his obstinacy.

The Indians were for peace; they had suffered sufficiently. Cornstalk upbraided his people because they had not listened to his suggestions of peace before the battle. "What," said he, "will you do now? The Big Knife is coming on us and we shall all be killed. Now you must fight, or we are undone." He paused for a reply. "Then let us kill all our women and children, and go and fight till we die." Still there was no answer. Rising, he struck his tomahawk sharply into a post of the council-house, exclaiming, "I'll go and make peace." The only response was a satisfactory "Ough! ough!" from the warriors.

Colonel Wilson, of Dunmore's staff, says of his oratory in the council:

"When he arose, he was no wise confused or daunted, but spoke in a distinct and audible voice, without stammering or repetition, and with peculiar emphasis. His looks, while addressing Dunmore, were truly grand and majestic, yet graceful and attractive. I have heard many celebrated orators, but never one whose powers of delivery surpassed those of Cornstalk on this occasion."

John Gibson, the interpreter to Lord Dunmore, stated in "Jefferson's Notes," that on his arrival at the towns, Logan, the Indian, came to where the deponent was sitting with Cornstalk and the other chiefs of the Shawnees, and asked him to walk out with him; that they went into a copse of wood, where they sat down, when Logan, after shedding abundance of tears, delivered to him the speech, nearly as related by Mr. Jefferson in his notes on the State of Virginia; that he, the deponent, told him that it was not Colonel Cresap who had murdered his relations, and that although his son, Captain Michael Cresap, was with the party that killed a Shawnese chief and other Indians, yet he was not present when his relations were killed at Baker's, near the mouth of Yellow Creek, on the Ohio; that this deponent, on his return to camp, delivered the speech to Lord Dunmore; and that the murders perpetrated as above were considered as ultimately the cause of the war of 1774, commonly called Cresap's war."

There are several versions of this remarkable speech, as reported by different authors. The following is the Jefferson version:

"I appeal to any white man to say if ever he entered Logan's cabin hungry, and he gave him not meat; if ever he came cold and naked, and he clothed him not. During the course of the last long and bloody war, Logan remained in his cabin, an advocate for peace. Such was my love for the whites, that my countrymen pointed as they passed, and said, 'Logan is the friend of white men.' I had even thought to have lived with you, but for the injuries of one man. Colonel Cresap, the last spring, in cold blood and unprovoked, murdered all the relations of Logan, not even sparing my women and children. There runs not a drop of my blood in the veins of any living creature. This called on me for revenge. I have sought it. I have killed many. I have fully glutted my vengeance For my country, I rejoice at the beams of peace. But do not harbor a thought that mine is the joy of fear. Logan never felt fear. He will not turn on his heel to save his life. Who is there to mourn for Logan? Not one."[*]

---

[*] From "Red Men of the Ohio Valley," p. 140 to 146.

# APPENDIX.

### THE SHADE OF LOGAN.— By Joseph D. Canning, Esq.

Through the wilds of the West, in the fall of the year,
A wanderer strayed in pursuit of the deer;
And clad in the garb of the hunter was he—
The moccasined foot, and the bead-gartered knee.

Though far towards the sunrise the wanderer's home,
He loved in the gardens of nature to roam;
By her melodies charmed, by her varying tale,
He followed through forest and prairie her trail.

By the shore of a river at sunset he strayed,
And lingered to rest 'neath a sycamore shade;
For soft was the breath of the summer-like air,
And the sweetest of scenes for a painter was there.

He mused: and in slumber the past was restored,
When thy waters, Scioto, a wilderness shored!
And the shade of a Mingo before him uprose—
The friend of the white man, the fear of his foes.

Erect and majestic his form as of yore;
The mists of the stream as a mantle he wore;
And o'er his dark bosom the bright wampum showed,
Like the hues of the bow on the folds of a cloud.

The tones of his voice were the accents of grief,
For gloomy and sad was the Shade of the Chief;
And low as the strain of the whispering shell
His words on the ear of the slumberer fell:—

"I appeal to the white man ungrateful, to say
If he e'er from my cabin went hungry away?
If naked and cold unto Logan he came,
And he gave him no blanket, and kindled no flame?

"When war, long and bloody, last deluged the land,
Not Logan was seen at the head of his band;
From his cabin he looked for the fighting to cease,
And, scorned by his brethren, wrought the wampum of peace.

"My love to the white man was steadfast and true,
Unlike the deep hatred my red brothers knew;
With him I had thought to have builded my home,
No more o'er the forest and prairie to roam.

"When the leaf which pale Autumn is withering now
Was fresh from its budding, and green on the bough,
Unprovoked, by the white man my kindred were slain,
And Logan became the wild Indian again!

"There runs not a drop of my blood in the veins
Of any who lives—not a mortal remains!
Not even my wife or my children were spared—
All alike at the hand of the murderer shared!

"This called for revenge, and to seek it I rose;
My hatchet is red with the blood of my foes,
The ghosts of the dead are appeased by their sire—
I have glutted my vengeance, and scorn to retire!

"I joy for my country that peace should appear,
But think not that mine is the gladness of fear.
Logan never felt fear. In the deadliest strife
He'll not turn on his heel for the saving of life.

# APPENDIX.

"Who is there to sorrow for Logan? Not one!"
Thus spoke, and the Shade of the Mingo was gone!
But LOGAN, thy words in his mem'ry are borne,
Who waking did mourn thee, and ever will mourn.*

EPITAPH FOR THE LOGAN MONUMENT.—By Jos. D. CANNING.

LOGAN! to thy memory here,
White men do this tablet rear;
On its front we grave thy name—
In our hearts shall live thy fame.

While Niagara's thunders roar;
Or Erie's surges lash the shore:
While onward broad Ohio glides,
And seaward roll her Indian tides,
So long *their* memory, who did give
These floods their sounding names, shall live.

While time, in kindness, buries low
The gory axe and warrior's bow,
O, Justice! faithful to thy trust,
Record the virtues of the just! †

NARRATIVE OF COLONEL ROBERT PATTERSON.

"In the fall of 1776, I started from McClellan's Station, (now Georgetown, Ky.), in company with Joseph M'Nutt, David Perry, James Wernock, James Templeton, Edward Mitchell, and Isaac Greer, to go to Pittsburg. We procured provisions

---
*From "Williams' American Pioneer," Vol. I, pp. 116 and 117.
†From "Williams' American Pioneer," Vol. II, p. 468.

for our journey at the Blue Licks, from the well-known stone house, the Buffalo. At Limestone, we procured a canoe, and started up the Ohio River by water. Nothing material transpired during several of the first days of our journey. We landed at Point Pleasant, where was a fort commanded by Captain Arbuckle. After remaining there a short time, and receiving dispatches from Captain Arbuckle for the commandant at Wheeling, we again proceeded. Aware that Indians were lurking along the bank of the river, we traveled with the utmost caution. We usually landed an hour before sunset, cooked and eat our supper, and went on until after dark. At night we lay without fire, as convenient to our canoe as possible, and started again in the morning at daybreak. We had all agreed that if any disaster should befall us, by day or night, that we would stand by each other, as long as any help could be afforded. At length the memorable 12th of October arrived. During the day we passed several new improvements, which occasioned us to be less watchful and careful than we had been before. Late in the evening we landed opposite the island (on the Ohio side of the river, in what is now Athens county), then called the Hockhocking, and were beginning to flatter ourselves that we should reach some inhabitants the next day. Having eaten nothing that day, contrary to our usual practice, we kindled a fire and cooked supper. After we had eaten and made the last of our flour into a loaf of bread, and put it into an old brass kettle to bake, that we might be ready to start again, in the morning, at daybreak, we lay down to rest, keeping the same clothes on at night that we wore during the day. For the want of a better, I had on a hunting shirt and a breech-clout (so called), and flannel leggins. I had my powder horn and shot pouch on my side, and placed the butt of my gun under my head. Five of our company lay on the east side of the fire, and James

Templeton and myself on the west; we were lying on our left sides, myself in front, with my right hand hold of my gun. Templeton was laying close behind me. This was our position, and asleep, when we were fired upon by a party of Indians. Immediately after the fire they rushed upon us with tomahawks, as if determined to finish the work of death they had begun. It appeared that one Indian had shot on my side of the fire. I saw the flash of the gun, and felt the ball pass through me, but where I could not tell, nor was it, at first, painful. I sprang to take up my gun, but my right shoulder came to the ground. I made another effort, and was half bent in getting up, when an Indian sprang past the fire with savage fierceness, and struck me with his tomahawk. From the position I was in, it went between two ribs, just behind the backbone, a little below the kidney, and penetrated the cavity of the body. He then immediately turned to Templeton (who, by this time, had got to his feet with his gun in hand), and sized his gun. A desperate scuffle ensued, but Templeton held on, and finally bore off the gun. In the meantime, I made from the light, and in my attempt to get out of sight, I was delayed for a moment by getting my right arm fast between a tree and a sapling, but having got clear and away from the light of the fire, and finding that I had lost the use of my right arm, I made a shift to keep it up by drawing it through the straps of my shot-pouch. I could see the crowd about the fire, but the firing had ceased, and the strife seemed to be over. I had reason to believe that the others were all shot and tomahawked. Hearing no one coming toward me, I resolved to go to the river, and if possible to get into the canoe and float down, thinking by that means I might possibly reach Point Pleasant, supposed to be about one hundred miles distant. Just as I got on the beach a little below the canoe, an Indian in the canoe gave a whoop, which gave me to understand that it was best to withdraw. I did so; and with much difficulty got to an old log, and being very thirsty, faint and exhausted, I was glad to sit down. I felt the blood running, and heard it dropping on the leaves all around me. Presently I heard the Indians board the canoe and float past. All was now silent, and I felt myself in a most forlorn condition; I could not see the fire, but determined to find it, and see if any of my comrades were alive. I steered the course which I supposed the fire to be, and having reached it, I found Templeton alive, but wounded in nearly the same manner that I was; James Wernock was also dangerously wounded, two balls having passed through his body; Joseph M'Nutt was dead and scalped; D. Perry was wounded, but not badly, and Isaac Greer was missing. The miseries of that hour cannot well be described.

"When daylight appeared we held a council, and concluded that inasmuch as one gun and some ammunition was saved, Perry would furnish us with meat, and we would proceed up the river by slow marches to the nearest settlements, supposed to be one hundred miles. A small quantity of provisions which was found scattered around the fire, was picked up and distributed among us, and a piece of blanket which was saved from the fire, was given to me to cover a wound in my back. On examination, it was found that two balls had passed through my right arm, and that the bone was broken; to dress this, splinters were taken from a tree near the fire, that had been shivered by lightning, and placed on the outside of my hunting-shirt, and bound with a string. And now being in readiness to move, Perry took the gun and ammunition, and we all got to our feet except Wernock, who, on attempting to get up, fell back to the ground. He refused to try again, said that he could not live, and at the same time desired us to do the best we could for ourselves. Perry then took hold of his arm, and told him that if he would get up he would carry him; upon this he made another effort to get up, but falling back as before, he begged us in the most solemn manner to leave him. At his request, the old kettle was filled with water and placed at his side, which he said was the last and only favor he required of us, and then conjured us to leave him and try to save ourselves, assuring us that should he live to see us again, he would cast no reflections of unkindness upon us. Thus we left him. When we had got a little distance I looked back, and distressed and hopeless as Wernock's condition really was, I felt to envy it. After going about one hundred poles, we were obliged to stop and rest, and found ourselves too sick and weak to proceed. Another consultation being held, it was agreed that Templeton and myself should remain there with Edward Mitchell, and Perry should take the gun and go to the nearest settlement and seek relief. Perry promised that if he could not procure assistance, he would be back in four days; he then returned to the camp and found Wernock in the same state of mind as when we left; perfectly rational and sensible of his condition; replenished his kettle with water, brought us some fire, and started for the settlement.

Alike unable to go back or forward, and being very thirsty we set about getting water from a small stream that happened to be near us, our only drinking vessel an old wool hat, which was so broken that it was with great difficulty made to hold water; but by stuffing leaves in it, we made it hold so that each one could drink from once filling it. Nothing could have been a greater luxury to us than a drink of water from the old hat. Just at night, Mitchell returned to see if Wernock was still living, intending if he was dead, to get the kettle for us; he arrived just in time to see him expire, but not choosing to leave him until he should be certain he was dead, he staid with him until darkness came on, and when he attempted to return to us, he got lost, and lay from us all night. We suffered much that night from want of fire, and through fear that he was either killed, or that he had run off; but happily for us our fears were groundless, for next morning at sunrise he found his way to our camp. That day we moved about two hundred yards further up a deep ravine, and further from the river. The weather, which had been cold and frosty, now became a little warmer and commenced raining. Those that were with me could set up, but I had no alternative but to lie on my back on the ground, with my right arm over my body. The rain continued next day. Mitchell took an excursion to examine the hills, and not far distant, he found a rock projecting from the cliff sufficiently to shelter us from the rain, to which place we very gladly removed; he also gathered pawpaws for us, which were our only food, except perhaps a few grapes.

"Time moved slowly on until Saturday. In the meantime, we talked over the dangers to which Perry was exposed, the distance he had to go, and the improbability of his returning. When the time had expired which he had allowed himself, we concluded that we would, if alive, wait for him until Monday, and if he did not come then, and no relief should be afforded, we would attempt to travel to Point Pleasant. The third day after our defeat my arm became very painful; the splinters and sleeves of my shirt were cemented together with blood, and stuck so fast to my arm that it required the application of warm water for nearly a whole day to loosen them so that they could be taken off; when this was done I had my arm dressed with white oak leaves, which had a very good effect. On Saturday, about 12 o'clock, Mitchell came with his bosom full of pawpaws, and placed them convenient to us, and returned to his station on the river. He had been gone about an hour, when to our great joy we beheld him coming with a company of men. When they approached us, we found that our trusty friend and companion, David Perry, had returned to our assistance with Captain John Walls, his officers and most of his company. Our feelings of gratitude may possibly be conceived, but words can never describe them. Suffice it to say that these eyes flowed down plenteously with tears, and I was so completely overwhelmed with joy that I fell to the ground. On my recovery, we were taken to the river and refreshed plentifully with provisions which the captain had brought, and had our wounds dressed by an experienced man, who came for that purpose. We were afterward described by the captain to be in a most forlorn and pitiable condition, more like corpses beginning to putrify, than living beings.

"While we were at the cliff which sheltered us from the rain, the howling of the wolves in the direction of the fatal spot whence we had so narrowly escaped with our lives, left no doubt that they were feasting on the bodies of our much lamented friends, M'Nutt and Wernock. While we were refreshing ourselves at the river, and having our wounds dressed, Captain Walls went with some of his men to the place of our defeat and collected the bones of our late companions, and buried them with the utmost expedition and care. We were then conducted by water to Captain Walls' station, at Grave Creek."

Colonel Patterson was the original proprietor of Lexington, Kentucky, and owner of one-third of the original town plot of Cincinnati. He was a celebrated Indian fighter; was with General Geo. Rogers Clark in his Illinois expedition of 1778; in Bowman's expedition against Old Chillicothe, in 1779; under Clark again in his memorable Mad River campaign of 1780; second to Colonel Boone at the battle of the Lower Blue Licks in 1782; a colonel under Clark in his Miami expedition of 1783; and in the

Shawnee expedition of Colonel Logan in 1786. He removed to the vicinity of Dayton in 1804, where he died, August 5, 1827.

*From "Red Men of the Ohio Valley," p. 175 to 183.*

www.ingramcontent.com/pod-product-compliance
Lightning Source LLC
Chambersburg PA
CBHW022143090426
42742CB00010B/1368